FEISTY FELTIES

FEISTY FELTIES

MISSY COVINGTON

REBEL CRAFTS FOR **BUDDING FEMINISTS**!

Skyhorse Publishing

Skyhorse Publishing books may be purchased in bulk at special discounts for sales promotion, corporate gifts, fund-raising, or educational purposes. Special editions can also be created to specifications. For details, contact the Special Sales Department, Skyhorse Publishing, 307 West 36th Street, 11th Floor, New York, NY 10018 or info@skyhorsepublishing.com.

Skyhorse® and Skyhorse Publishing® are registered trademarks of Skyhorse Publishing, Inc.®, a Delaware corporation.

Visit our website at www.skyhorsepublishing.com.

10 9 8 7 6 5 4 3 2 1

Library of Congress Cataloging-in-Publication Data is available on file.

Cover design by Leah Germann
Cover photo credit Missy Covington

Print ISBN: 978-1-5107-4809-5
Ebook ISBN: 978-1-5107-4895-8

Printed in China

Contents

Tools & Materials

All you need to complete the projects in this book are a few basic craft and sewing tools. These are readily available at craft, hobby, and fabric stores, or online retailers.

TOOLS

Sharp fabric scissors: These are critical for cutting felt, which may develop loose fibers at the edges if cut with a blunt blade.

Paper scissors: You'll need a pair of craft or paper scissors to cut out the paper pattern pieces. Do not use fabric scissors to cut paper—it will dull the blades very quickly.

Hot glue gun and hot glue sticks: Hot glue is superior to other types of fabric glue as it bonds the felt securely and dries extremely fast. I prefer high-temperature hot glue guns as they give you slightly more time to reposition or work with your piece. However, low-temperature hot glue guns might be a better choice for younger crafters.

Embroidery needles: These come in a variety of different sizes. You'll need a finer needle to stitch some detail work that uses fewer strands of embroidery floss (i.e. face detail), while more strands of embroidery floss require a larger eye and don't need a fine needle. Get a 5/10 size variety pack.

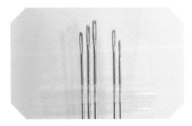

WHY NOT TRY?
Make your projects your own by incorporating sequins, feathers, glitter, and more. Don't have gold cord for Frida's necklace? Try a string of plastic beads, ribbon, yarn, or even a spare necklace. You can also incorporate real fabric pieces for additional detail.

Paper: Trace or copy the pattern pieces from the book onto standard weight printer paper. If you wish, you can use tracing or pattern paper instead. Avoid using heavier weight paper as it will be difficult to trace and stitch through.

Tape: Taping the pattern pieces to the felt before cutting out the felt makes it easy to get great, precise results without them slipping. I use matte "invisible" tape.

Tweezers: These are optional, but they are useful when placing small pieces of felt and will protect your fingertips when hot-gluing pieces together. I prefer fine-point, curved tip tweezers.

MATERIALS

Acrylic felt: The felt used in these projects is ⅝ in.– (1.5mm-) thick acrylic felt that is available in either bolts or sheets (usually 9 x 12 in./22.8 x 30.5cm or 12 x 12 in./30.5 x 30.5cm) at fabric and craft stores, or online. (See page 8.)

Embroidery floss: This acrylic or cotton thread is sold in skeins. It is comprised of six individual threads twisted together. For some projects, you will need only two or three of the threads. To separate them, cut an 18 in. (45.7cm) length of thread and separate one end so you can see the strands. One at a time, carefully pull out the number of strands you need, then hold them together and run your fingers along them so that they combine to make a single thread.

SCALING THE PATTERN PIECES

Some pattern pieces in this book are true-to-size (shown at 100 percent) and some need to be scaled up before you use them. Each pattern notes whether it is scaled (and by what percentage) or if it is true to size.

- The true-to-size pattern pieces can be traced or photocopied directly from the book.

- To enlarge a pattern piece from the book to full size, use a photocopier to print the piece at the percentage noted.

- Alternatively, you can scan the pattern pieces into a computer and then print them out at the noted percentage.

Types of Felt

Felt is a versatile craft material. Depending on the thickness, stiffness, and fiber composition, it allows you to add fine detail, make sturdy utility items, and create washable fashion pieces.

Felt is available in synthetic (acrylic) or natural (wool) fibers. Acrylic felt is the most common type. It is available in a variety of densities and thicknesses. This felt is hand washable without shrinkage. Acrylic is a good all-purpose felt, and is generally a more economical choice—especially for beginning crafters. For most of the projects in this book, soft acrylic felt is the best material as it is suitable for cutting out fine details, and can be used to show stitch details. This felt is readily available in bolts and sheets in craft stores.

Stiff (often thin) acrylic felt is fantastic for rendering very fine details (like lettering or small intricate objects). However, it can also be more difficult to sew through for fine stitch detailing. Wool felt tends to have denser fibers, greater thickness, and a more luxe feel. Although wool felt is naturally water resistant, it may shrink if it gets wet and is damaged if submerged in water. Wool felt is suitable for projects that require denser, thicker felt but that don't need fine detail stitching. For example, the coin purse (see page 60) can be made in wool felt for extra durability.

ASK AN ADULT
If you need help with any of the steps, such as threading a needle, using scissors, or a glue gun ask an adult.

CUTTING OUT THE FELT PIECES

Although felt does not fray, cutting a very small piece can cause the fibers at the edges to become loose. (The denser the felt, the less of a problem this is.) For the best results:

• Use very sharp fabric scissors.

• Tape down your pattern pieces to your felt—but be careful when removing the tape so as not to snag a small piece of felt.

• If you need to cut out more than one piece of a particular shape, you may cut through multiple layers of felt. However, the felt is prone to slipping, so watch that one piece does not end up smaller than the other one.

Gluing

The majority of the projects in this book utilize hot glue from a glue gun. It sets quickly but using it takes practice. However, the benefits—great bonding, rapid setting, precision placement, no matting of the felt—outweigh the disadvantages. Take care not to burn your fingers. Once set, the glue is essentially permanent.

Ultra-low temperature glue guns designed for kids offer similar benefits to high-temperature models without the risk of burned fingertips. However, the glue dries faster.

Things to note:

- Glue from a gun will leave little "threads" of glue that will need to be peeled or snipped off the project once the glue has dried.

- Do not use glue in a place that you're going to stitch through later. It will be difficult to get the needle through the glue.

Hot Glue Alternatives

If you do not wish to use hot glue, you may:

- Stitch on pieces instead of gluing

- Use tacky glue, such as school or PVA

- Use fabric glue

If you use other glues, you will need to take breaks in between steps to let the glue dry before moving to the next step.

HOT GLUE SAFETY

Please refer to the manufacturer's warnings when using a hot glue gun. Some project specific safety tips:

- Using tweezers (see page 7) to place small felt pieces reduces the risk of burned fingertips.

- You may wear fingertip covers (available at hobby stores) if you feel less confident about your glue prowess. This may, however, make you a little clumsy.

- Do not leave your glue gun on overnight.

Finishing

When sewing two layers of felt together, start the first stitch and complete the last stitch between the two layers, instead of at the back of the piece. This will allow you to hide the thread ends between the layers.

When you have finished stitching, you can leave the ends as they are, tie them in a knot (either tie two ends or make a knot in a single strand that is substantial enough not to pull through the felt), or use glue to secure them. If you're not worried how the back of a piece looks, the ends can be glued down on the back of your project.

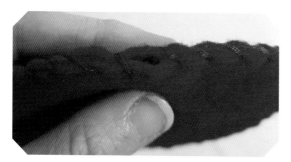

If you want a neater finish, you can tuck in your ends between the layers of felt and make a small "pocket" for the nozzle of the glue gun. Insert the gun, squeeze in a small amount of glue and press the pieces together to secure your final stitches.

USING DIFFERENT TECHNIQUES

In many cases, the projects in this book can be modified to make them simpler, use different skills, or add embellishments. For example, to save time and make projects easier to complete use fabric paint instead of stitches for the details, or use glue instead of stitching to join seams. For projects with a lot of fine details, increase the pattern size so that you can use larger stitches and a thicker embroidery floss. Alternatively, up the skill level by stitching all the details rather than using fabric paint.

Embroidery Stitches

The projects in this book use six different embroidery stitches.

BACKSTITCH

The backstitch produces a smooth, straight line and is used for most precise detailing.

1 From the back of the felt, bring your needle up to the front one stitch ahead of where you want to start.

2 Pull your thread through (leaving a short tail for the first stitch) and stitch back to where you'd like to start. Push your needle through the front of the felt to the back.

3 Pull your thread through to the back, then position your needle ahead of your next stitch and bring it through the felt.

4 Go back to the previous stitch and use the same hole to create an unbroken line.

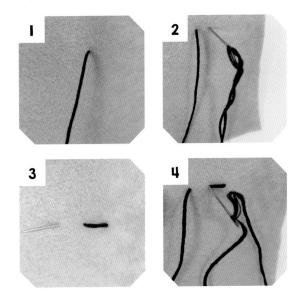

RUNNING STITCH

The running stitch is simple, quick, and is used mostly for decorative stitches.

1 From the back of the felt, bring your needle up at the point where you want your stitch to begin.

2 From the front, push your needle back through the felt at the desired length of your stitch.

3 Repeat, using an even spacing and bringing your needle up at the beginning of a stitch and back down at the end of a stitch.

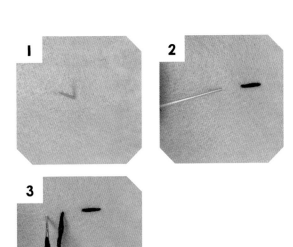

DOUBLE RUNNING STITCH

This is a simple way to create a line that looks the same on the front and back of a project.

1 Create a line of running stitches. Here the stitches follow a line marked on the pattern.

2 Double back and complete a second row of running stitches, filling in the gaps you left with the first stitch to create a solid line.

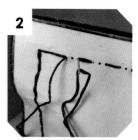

FRENCH KNOT

The French knot creates a knot on the top of the fabric.

1 Bring your needle through the back of your felt to the front just slightly beside your desired French knot position.

2 Keeping the thread firmly in hand, loop the slack thread around your needle twice.

3 Keeping the looped strand tight on your needle, hold the slack so that it doesn't slip or bunch, and push your needle (with the looped strands) through the felt at the exact point of your desired French knot.

4 Pull the needle and thread through the felt so that the knot sits on the surface.

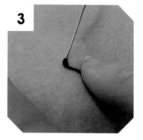

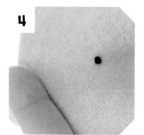

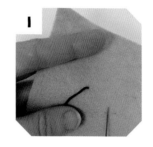

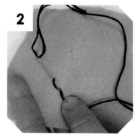

OVERCAST STITCH

This is a simple edging stitch that is great for attaching layers. This creates a diagonal look around the edge of your piece.

1 Bring your needle through from the back of your felt to the front.

2 Go around the edge of the piece and bring the needle through from the back of your felt to the front again at the desired interval.

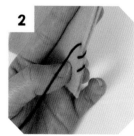

BLANKET STITCH

This is an edging stitch that has a very distinct look. It is very important to keep your stitches even when utilizing a blanket stitch.

1 Bring your needle from the back to the front of the felt, then re-insert it into the back, creating a loop.

2 Bring your needle through the loop, coming from the inside of the loop away from the direction you want to stitch.

3 At your desired interval, take over needle and loop from back to front, leaving a bit of loop slack.

4 Before tightening your stitch, bring your needle through that loop.

5 Tighten and move onto the next stitch using the same technique.

6 Continue to stitch along the seam, making sure all of the stitches are an even size.

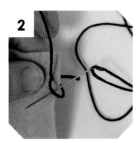

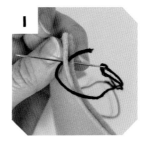

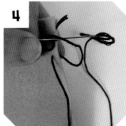

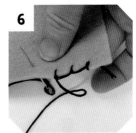

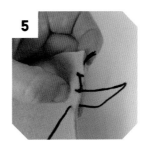

ADDING STITCHED DETAILS

The paper pattern pieces are used as a guide when adding the stitched details. Stitch through the paper and the felt, but keep the stitches small to make the paper easier to remove later. When you're ready to remove the paper, carefully tear it away from the stitches, being carefully not to pull at them or they may pop out of the fabric. You may find it helpful to dampen the paper with a little water from a sponge or spray bottle first. Use tweezers to pull out any small, stubborn pieces of paper.

CLEANING FELT

Acrylic felt may be washed/submerged, but hand-washing is recommended to preserve details. Use warm water and gentle soap. Some fiber flyaway may occur. Acrylic pieces may be dried on low heat in a dryer, though air-drying is preferred. The hot glue used in these pieces should be hand-washed and may detach under vigorous agitation.

The Projects

Notable women have the power to change the world, to capture our imaginations, and to inspire us to set our own goals and dreams higher and bigger than before. Turn the page to discover projects featuring some of the feistiest women and girls and let them influence and motivate you—from contemporaries, to historical figures, to goddesses. There are also projects that will allow you to capture your own spirit of innovation and persistence—and remind you how powerful you truly are. Write with Maya, act out with Frida, dream with Pele the fire goddess, show your allyship, set your own goals and dreams, and revel in the functional strength of your own body. Get out your felt and get ready to spark your creativity and shake up the status quo.

Difficulty Ratings

★ **Easy**

★★ **Average**

★★★ **Expert**

Frida Kahlo Puppet

Playact with a hand puppet of inspirational painter Frida Kahlo, who was one of Mexico's premiere artists.

Frida Kahlo was known for her trail-blazing self-portraits and her bold, unflinching style that incorporated the natural beauty of Mexico and a heavy dash of imagination.

TOOLS & MATERIALS

- 24 x 8 in. (61 x 20.3cm) tan felt
- 9 x 8 in. (22.9 x 20.3cm) black felt
- 7 x 6 in. (17.8 x 15.2cm) yellow felt
- 9 x 5 in. (22.9 x 12.7cm) dark brown felt
- 2½ x 1½ in. (6.3 x 3.8cm) green felt
- 4 x 2 in. (10.2 x 5.1cm) pink felt
- 3 x 2 in. (7.6 x 5.1cm) dark pink felt
- 13 in. (33cm) neckline embellishment
- 13 in. (33cm) hemline embellishment

- 8 in. (20.3cm) and 12 in. (30.5cm) necklace material
- Red embroidery floss
- Black embroidery floss
- Tan embroidery floss
- Paper
- Paper scissors

- Sewing scissors
- Tape
- Embroidery needles
- Hot glue gun and hot glue sticks
- Tweezers (optional)

1 Photocopy the pattern pieces onto paper and cut them out. Do not cut along the inner lines on the shirt or skirt hem—these are a guide for the embellishments. Tape the pattern pieces to the felt using the colors stated. Cut out all the pieces except the face.

2 Use the backstitch (see page 11) and red embroidery floss to add the mouth detail to the face. Use the backstitch and black embroidery floss to add the eye and nose detail to the face. Cut out the face. Remove the pattern pieces.

3 Use the overcast stitch (see page 12) and tan embroidery floss to stitch the body pieces together, leaving the base open.

4 Assemble the face by gluing the sections together as follows: the hair to the head; the eyes to the face; then glue on the eyebrows. You can use tweezers to help you if you like (see page 7).

5 Glue the back of the head to the back of the puppet—lay down the back head piece, apply glue to the center, and put the puppet on top of it to ensure it remains in the correct direction.

6 Glue the face piece on top of the puppet and to the back head piece.

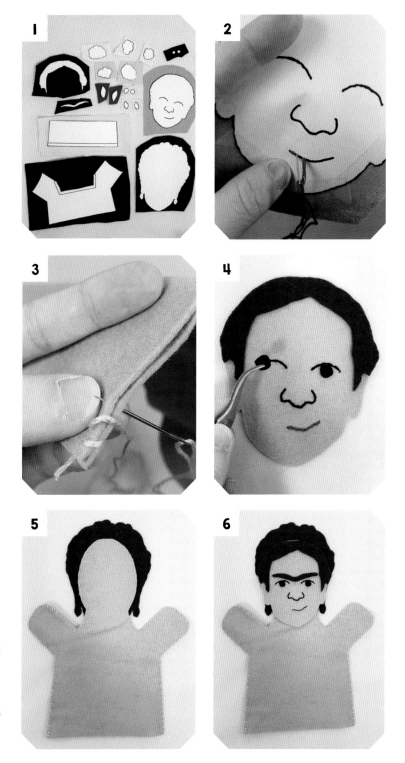

Frida Kahlo Puppet

7 Glue on the flowers in this order: the two back flowers, then the middle flower, and finally the two front flowers. Add the centers of the front flowers, then the two leaf pieces at the point where the front and back of the head meet. Glue on the earrings.

8 Add the clothes: Glue the yellow skirt pieces to the front and back of the puppet. Put a small dab of glue at the seam on the side and pinch the two skirt pieces together at the sides.

9 Glue the black shirt pieces to the front and back of the puppet—it will overlap the skirt. Put a small dab of glue at the seams on the sides and pinch the two shirt pieces together.

10 Glue the embellishment to the front and back neckline of the shirt. Repeat for the skirt hemline. Glue two strands of necklace embellishment to the back of the puppet.

You can use whatever materials you have on hand to decorate the hem and neckline of Frida's clothing and necklace. For the hems we used red rick-rack, but you may use a strip of ribbon, fabric, or lace. And for the necklace we used holiday wrapping cord, but you may want to try yarn, ribbon, bead strings, or tinsel.

Pattern Pieces

FINISHED SIZE: 9 x 10½ in. (22.9 x 26.7cm)

Pattern pieces shown at 40 percent. Photocopy at 250 percent to enlarge them to full size (see page 7).

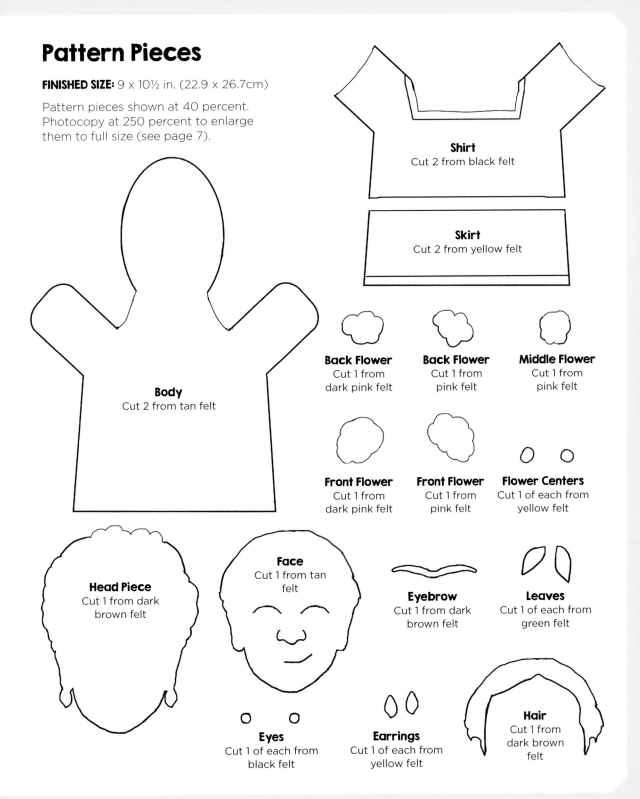

Shirt
Cut 2 from black felt

Skirt
Cut 2 from yellow felt

Body
Cut 2 from tan felt

Back Flower
Cut 1 from dark pink felt

Back Flower
Cut 1 from pink felt

Middle Flower
Cut 1 from pink felt

Front Flower
Cut 1 from dark pink felt

Front Flower
Cut 1 from pink felt

Flower Centers
Cut 1 of each from yellow felt

Head Piece
Cut 1 from dark brown felt

Face
Cut 1 from tan felt

Eyebrow
Cut 1 from dark brown felt

Leaves
Cut 1 of each from green felt

Eyes
Cut 1 of each from black felt

Earrings
Cut 1 of each from yellow felt

Hair
Cut 1 from dark brown felt

Pele Pillow

Add fiery flare to your bedroom with a pillow decorated with the image of Pele—the Hawaiian goddess of volcanoes and fire.

Pele represents female power, passion, and strength. Her full name—Pelehonuamea—means "she who shapes the sacred land," and she is said to live in the Halemaʻumaʻu Crater at the Hawaii Volcanoes National Park.

TOOLS & MATERIALS

- 15 x 7½ in. (38.1 x 19cm) dark gray felt
- 9½ x 4¼ in. (24.1 x 10.8cm) yellow felt
- 9½ x 3½ in. (24.1 x 8.9cm) orange felt
- 8½ x 4¼ in. (21.6 x 10.8cm) black felt
- 8½ x 4¼ in. (21.6 x 10.8cm) light brown felt

- 4½ x 3½ in. (11.4 x 8.9cm) red felt
- 2 x ½ in. (5.1 x 1.3cm) green felt
- Polyester toy stuffing
- Dark gray embroidery floss
- Black embroidery floss
- Red embroidery floss
- Paper

- Paper scissors
- Tape
- Sewing scissors
- Embroidery needles
- Hot glue gun and hot glue sticks
- Tweezers (optional)

1 Photocopy the pattern pieces onto paper and cut them out. Tape the pattern pieces to the felt, using the colors stated. Cut out all the pieces except the face.

2 Stitch the pillow base layers together 1 in. (2.5cm) from the edge on three sides using the double running stitch and dark gray embroidery floss. You can use the broken rule on the pattern piece as a guide. Start by working the running stitch (see page 11) around three sides. Then "double back" and work the running stitch along the seam, working in the opposite direction.

3 Take a few handfuls of polyester toy stuffing and stuff your pillow, making it as firm as you desire.

4 Use the double running stitch to stitch the fourth side together.

5 To add the details to the face, use the backstitch (see page 11) and black embroidery floss to sew the eye and nose details. Then use the backstitch and red embroidery floss to sew the lip detail. Remove the pattern pieces.

6 To assemble the body, glue the face to the body piece and then the dress to the body piece.

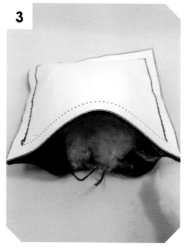

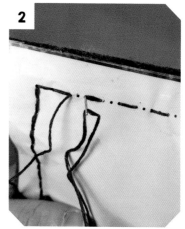

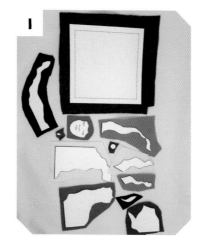

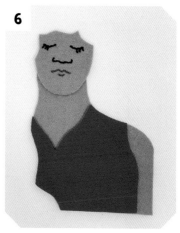

Pele Pillow

7 To assemble the hair, glue the black and orange hair streaks to the main yellow hair piece.

8 Glue the hair to the pillow, aligning the bottom corner with the stitched seam.

9 Glue the body piece to the pillow, aligning the base with the bottom pillow seam. Then glue the hair to the pillow.

10 Glue the three leaves to the hair so that they overlap. You can use tweezers to help you if you like (see page 7). Glue the flower onto the leaves as shown in the photograph.

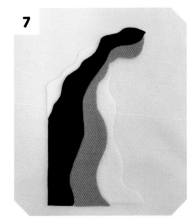

Pattern Pieces

FINISHED SIZE: 7 x 7 in (17.8 x 17.8cm)

Pattern pieces shown at 30 percent. Photocopy at 333 percent to enlarge them to full size (see page 7).

This pattern makes a small accent pillow. You may enlarge the pattern pieces for a bigger pillow, or purchase a pillow and glue an enlarged appliqué to it.

Pillow base
Cut 2 from dark gray felt

Base hair
Cut 1 from yellow felt

Center hair
Cut 1 from black felt

Hair streak
Cut 1 from orange felt

Hair streak
Cut 1 from orange felt

Hair streak
Cut 1 from black felt

Hair streak
Cut 1 from orange felt

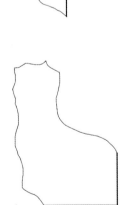

Body
Cut 1 from light brown felt

Dress
Cut 1 from red felt

Face
Cut 1 from light brown felt

Flower
Cut 1 from red felt

Leaves
Cut 3 from green felt

My Strong Body

Your body is a strong, wondrous thing—no matter what it looks like. Go inside: Explore deeper and celebrate its capabilities and biology.

Make sure that your heart is in the right place (not to mention your kidneys, uterus, and spleen) by placing twelve of your internal organs in position inside the body cavity.

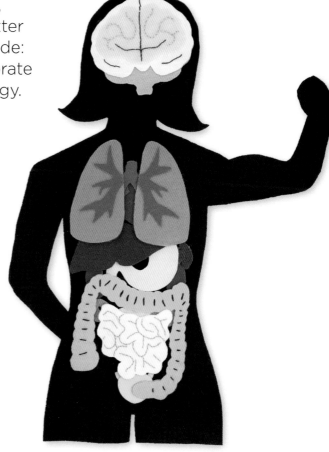

TOOLS & MATERIALS

- 24 x 18 in. (61 x 45.7cm) black felt
- 12 x 7 in. (30.5 x 17.7cm) blue felt
- 9 x 6½ in. (22.9 x 16.5cm) dark pink felt
- 13 x 6¼ in. (33 x 15.9cm) salmon felt
- 9 x 6 in. (22.9 x 15.2cm) cream pink felt
- 6 x 5½ in. (15.2 x 14cm) light gray felt
- 6½ x 5 in. (16.5 x 12.7cm) medium pink felt
- 6¼ x 5 in. (15.9 x 12.7cm) dark red felt
- 14½ x 4½ in. (36.8 x 11.4cm) light pink felt
- 8 x 3 in. (20.3 x 7.6cm) red felt

- 4 x 2½ in. (10.2 x 6.3cm) yellow felt
- 2 x 1½ in. (5.1 x 3.8cm) maroon felt
- 14 x ½-in. (35.6cm x 1.3cm) hook-and-loop fastener tape cut into 1 in. (2.5cm) strips
- Dark gray embroidery floss
- Light gray embroidery floss
- Dark pink embroidery floss

- Black embroidery floss
- Paper
- Paper scissors
- Tape
- Sewing scissors
- Embroidery needles
- Hot glue gun and hot glue sticks
- Tweezers (optional)

1 Photocopy the pattern pieces onto paper and cut them out, but do not cut along the dotted reference lines. On the paper body pattern only, cut out the marks for the positions of the hook-and-loop tape. Tape the pattern pieces to the felt, using the colors stated.

2 Secure the hook side of the 14 strips of hook-and-loop tape in the positions shown on the body pattern using a dab of glue in the center of each piece of tape.

3 Use the backstitch (see page 11) to add the stitched details to the brain, small, and large intestines. For the brain, use dark gray embroidery floss to stitch the detail onto the middle brain layer and the mid-line detail onto the top brain layer; and use light gray embroidery floss to stitch the remaining brain detail. For the small intestine, use dark pink embroidery floss to stitch the detail on the front intestine piece. For the large intestine, use black embroidery floss to stitch the detail on the front colon piece.

4 Cut out the remaining pieces of felt and remove the pattern pieces. Glue the back of the loop sides of the 1 in. (2.5cm) strips of hook-and-loop tape to the back of the base pieces in the position marked on the pattern pieces.

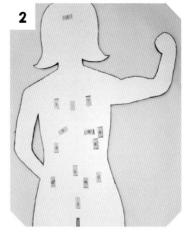

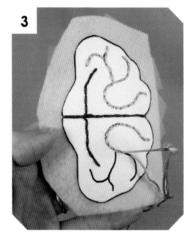

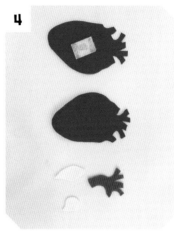

My Strong Body

5 To complete the bladder, glue the base and top pieces together (making sure that the hook-and-loop tape faces out).

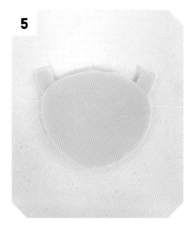

6 To complete the brain, glue the top piece to the middle piece, then the top and middle pieces to the base (making sure that the hook-and-loop tape faces out).

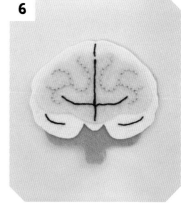

7 To complete the heart, glue the base and top pieces together (making sure that the hook-and-loop tape faces out). Glue the arteries and additional detail to the front of the heart. You can use tweezers to help you if you like (see page 7).

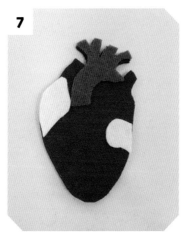

8 To complete the kidneys, glue the base and top pieces together (making sure that the hook-and-loop tape faces out).

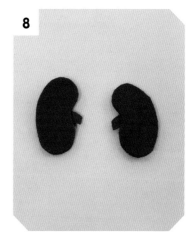

9 To complete the lungs, glue the base and top pieces together (making sure that the hook-and-loop tape faces out). Glue the arteries to the front of the lungs.

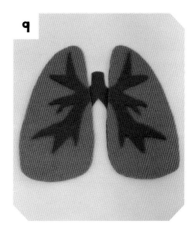

10 To complete the large intestine, glue the base and top pieces together (making sure that the hook-and-loop tape faces out).

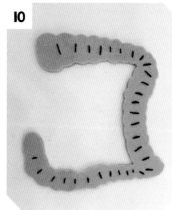

11 To complete the liver, glue the base and top pieces together (making sure that the hook-and-loop tape faces out).

12 To complete the stomach, glue the base and top pieces together (making sure that the hook-and-loop tape faces out).

13 To complete the small intestine, glue the base and top pieces together (making sure that the hook-and-loop tape faces out).

14 To complete the spleen, trim the hook-and-loop tape to fit the spleen. Glue the base and top pieces together (making sure that the hook-and-loop tape faces out).

15 To complete the uterus, glue the ovaries and cervical lining pieces to the top of the base piece (making sure that the hook-and-loop tape faces out). You can use tweezers to help you if you like (see page 7).

16 Affix all your organs to the body in the correct places.

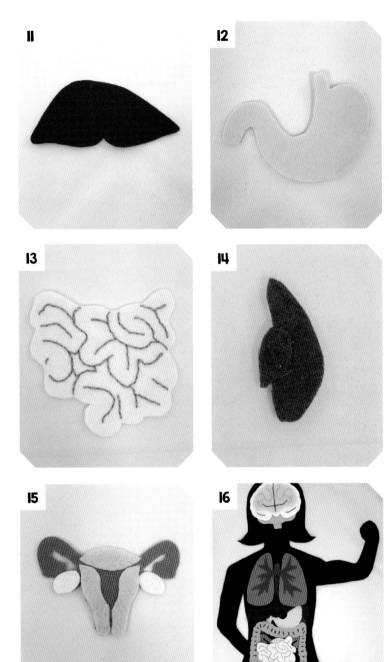

11

12

13

14

15

16

My Strong Body

Pattern Pieces

FINISHED SIZE: 17¼ x 23 in. (43.8 x 58.4cm)

Pattern pieces shown at 20 percent.
Photocopy at 500 percent to enlarge
them to full size (see page 7).

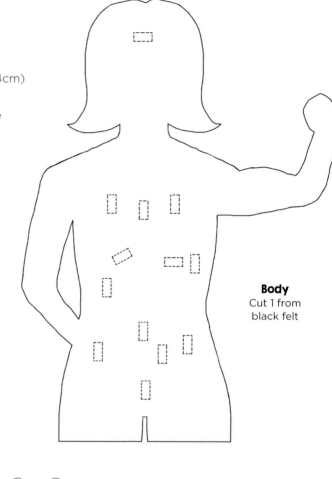

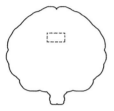

Brain base
Cut 1 from
light gray felt

Brain middle layer
Cut 1 from
cream pink felt

Brain top layer
Cut 1 from medium
pink felt

Body
Cut 1 from
black felt

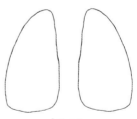

Lung base
Cut 1 from blue felt

Lungs
Cut 1 of each from
dark pink felt

Lung arteries
Cut 1 of each
from blue felt

Large intestine
Cut 1 of each from salmon felt

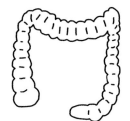

Uterus base
Cut 1 from dark pink felt

Small intestine
Cut 1 of each from light pink felt

Cervical lining
Cut 1 of each from light pink felt

Liver
Cut 1 of each from dark red felt

Ovaries
Cut 1 of each from cream pink felt

Stomach
Cut 1 of each from light pink felt

Spleen
Cut 1 of each from maroon felt

Kidneys base
Cut 2 of each from red felt

Kidneys top
Cut 2 of each from red felt

Heart base
Cut 1 of each from red felt

Heart arteries
Cut 1 of each from blue felt

Bladder base
Cut 1 from yellow felt

Bladder top
Cut 1 from yellow felt

Heart detail
Cut 1 of each from light pink felt

Goal Tree

Set goals and keep them in sight with this colorful goal tree.

Read a book, perform an act of kindness, get a good grade on an important test, win the debate... Change your goals as often as you achieve them, and use this as a visual reminder to keep climbing and growing.

TOOLS & MATERIALS

- 26 x 24 in. (66 x 61cm) white felt
- 20 x 13 in. (50.8 x 33cm) brown felt
- 8 x 6 in. (20.3 x 15.2cm) light green felt
- 8 x 4½ in. (20.3 x 11.4cm) dark green felt
- 8 x 4½ in. (20.3 x 11.4cm) medium green felt
- 4½ x 3½ in. (11.4 x 8.9cm) golden yellow felt
- 4 x 3½ in. (10.2 x 8.9cm) black felt
- 4 x 2 in. (10.2 x 5.1cm) yellow felt
- 4 x 2 in. (10.2 x 5.1cm) red felt
- 2½ x 2½ in. (6.3 x 6.3cm) dark gray felt

- 1 x ½ in. (2.5 x 1.3cm) orange felt
- 20 x 16 in. (50.8 x 40.6cm) cardboard or mat from a 20 x 16 in. (50.8 x 40.6cm) photo frame
- Photo frame with a 20 x 16 in. (50.8 x 40.6cm) opening (optional)
- Medium green embroidery floss
- Light green embroidery floss
- Dark green embroidery floss
- Seven ¼ in. (0.6cm) eyelets
- 3 in. (7.6cm) yellow yarn

- Seven 6 in. (15.2cm) lengths green yarn
- Gold fabric paint
- Red fabric paint
- Black fabric paint
- Paper
- Paper scissors
- Tape
- Sewing scissors
- Embroidery needles
- Hot glue gun and hot glue sticks
- Tweezers (optional)

1 Photocopy the pattern pieces onto paper and cut them out. Tape the pattern pieces to the felt using the colors stated.

2 To make the background, cut out a 24 x 20 in. (61 x 50.8cm) piece of white felt; center it on the piece of cardboard and turn the corners to the back of the cardboard. Glue to the back so that the felt is tight across the cardboard.

3 Cut out the tree and glue to the front of the white felt background. Cut out the leaves and goal icons. For the leaves with a hole marking, cut a small slit about ⅜ in. (0.7cm) at the position marked on the pattern piece. Remove the pattern pieces.

4 Use the backstitch (see page 11) and the color of embroidery floss listed to stitch the leaf details: medium green embroidery floss for the dark green leaves; light green embroidery floss for the medium green leaves; and dark green embroidery floss for the light green leaves.

5 Following the package instructions, attach the eyelets to the seven leaves with holes in them.

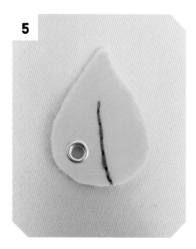

Goal Tree

6 Glue the leaves onto the tree and white background. Glue the plain leaves down completely. For the eyelet leaves, only glue the half of the leaf without an eyelet so that the yarn can be threaded through the eyelet.

7 Glue a length of green yarn to the inside of the base pieces of each of the goal icons so that it is in the center of each one.

8 To complete the saxophone, glue the top piece onto the base piece. Glue on key detail. You can use tweezers to help you if you like (see page 7).

9 To complete the graduation cap, glue the yellow yarn onto the right side of the cap. Glue the top mortar board piece onto the base cap piece.

10 To complete the heart, glue the top piece onto the base piece.

11 To complete the star, glue the top piece onto the base piece.

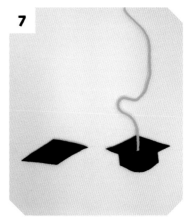

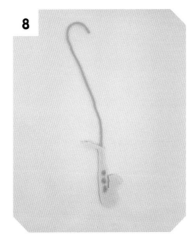

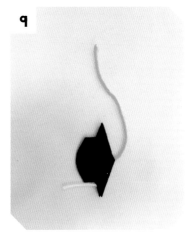

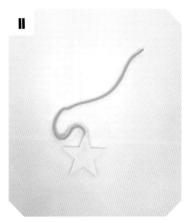

12 To complete the gavel, glue the top piece onto the base piece. Use the gold fabric paint to embellish the gavel head.

13 To complete the ball, glue the top piece onto the base piece. Use the red fabric paint to embellish the ball.

14 To complete the book, glue the top piece onto the base piece. Use the black fabric paint to embellish the book.

15 Hang your goal icons onto your tree using the lengths of yarn to tie them to the eyelets. You can frame the tree if you wish.

12
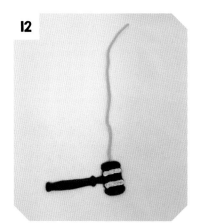

13
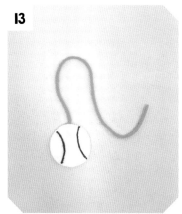

14

15

Set your own goals! Try making your own icons to represent your own targets, for example an actor's mask for memorizing a script, or a doctor symbol for learning first aid—your imagination is the only limit to your aspirations.

Goal Tree

Pattern Pieces

FINISHED SIZE:

20 x 16 in. (50.8 x 40.6cm)

Pattern pieces shown at 30 percent.
Photocopy at 333 percent to enlarge
them to full size (see page 7).

**Leaves with
a hole**
Cut 1 from dark
green felt,
3 from medium
green felt, and
4 from light
green felt

Leaves
Cut 10 from dark
green felt, 7 from
medium green felt,
and 10 from light
green felt

Heart
Cut 2 from
red felt

Ball
Cut 2 from
white felt

Book pages
Cut 1 from
white felt

Book base
Cut 1 from
dark gray felt

Star
Cut 2 from
yellow felt

Saxophone keys
Cut 1 of each from
orange felt

Saxophone body
Cut 2 from golden
yellow felt

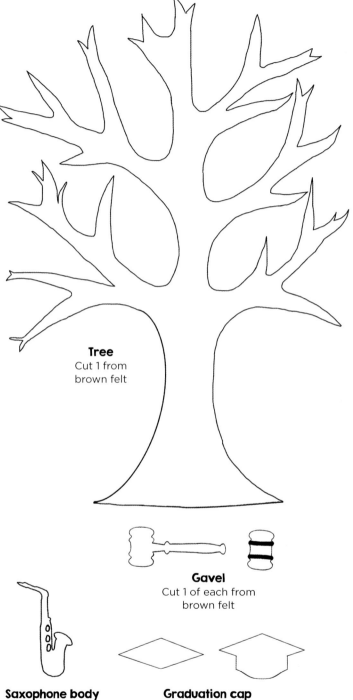

Tree
Cut 1 from
brown felt

Gavel
Cut 1 of each from
brown felt

Graduation cap
Cut 1 of each from
black felt

Ally Bracelet

Simple to make, these bracelets can be glued together for a minutes-long project, or you can add more decorative flair with stitching. The pattern is shown in two sizes—6 in. (15.2cm) for a looser fit, or 5 in. (12.7cm).

Show your true colors, express your identity, show what you stand for and who you stand with. Let friends know you're a safe space and a harbor of equality in a subtle, stylish way with these ally bracelets.

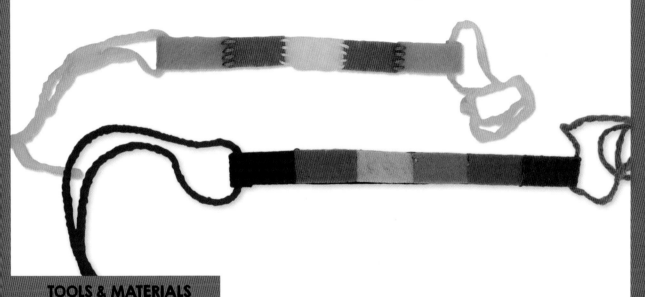

TOOLS & MATERIALS

For the Rainbow Ally Bracelet:
- 6½ x 1 in. (16.5 x 2.5cm) black felt
- 1¾ x 1 in. (4.5 x 2.5cm) red felt
- 1¾ x 1 in. (4.5 x 2.5cm) purple felt
- 1¼ x 1 in. (3.2 x 2.5cm) orange felt
- 1¼ x 1 in. (3.2 x 2.5cm) yellow felt
- 1¼ x 1 in. (3.2 x 2.5cm) green felt
- 1¼ x 1 in. (3.2 x 2.5cm) blue felt
- Two 10 in. (25.4cm) lengths of yarn

For the Trans Ally Bracelet:
- 6½ x 1 in. (16.5 x 2.5cm) white felt
- 3½ x 1 in. (8.9 x 2.5cm) turquoise felt
- 2½ x 1 in. (6.3 x 2.5cm) pink felt
- White embroidery floss

- Pink embroidery floss
- Two 10 in. (25.4cm) lengths of yarn
- Embroidery needles

For both bracelets
- Paper
- Paper scissors
- Tape
- Sewing scissors
- Hot glue gun and hot glue sticks

Rainbow Ally Bracelet

1 Photocopy the pattern pieces onto paper and cut them out, but do not cut along the dotted reference lines. Tape the pattern pieces to the felt, using the colors stated and cut them out. Remove the pattern pieces.

2 Place the red piece on top of the black piece so that 1 in. (2.5cm) of the red felt is on the base and ½ in. (1.3cm) hangs over the edge. Glue them together.

3 Repeat step 2 to glue the following pieces to the black base piece in this order: orange, yellow, green, blue, and purple (the purple felt, like the red, will hang ½ in. (1.3cm) over the base).

4 Place the centers of the 10 in. (25.4cm) lengths of yarn (shown here in red and purple) on the underside of the bracelet on the ends that hang over.

5 Glue the yarn to the ends of the bracelet and roll over the edges of the red and purple felt to secure them. Tie the yarn ends together so that the bracelet fits your wrist.

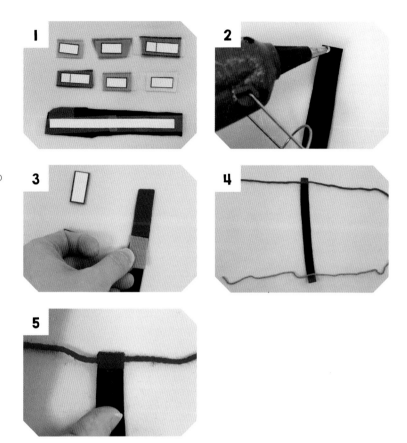

Pattern Pieces

FINISHED SIZE: 6 x ½ in. (15.2 x 1.3cm)

Pattern pieces shown at 50 percent. Photocopy at 200 percent to enlarge them to full size (see page 7).

End section Cut 1 from red felt and 1 from purple felt

Center section
Cut 1 each from yellow, orange, green, and blue felt

Base Cut 1 from black felt

Trans Ally Bracelet

1 Photocopy the pattern pieces onto paper and cut them out, but do not cut along the dotted reference lines. Tape the pattern pieces to the felt, using the colors stated and cut them out. Remove the pattern pieces.

2 Use the overcast stitch (see page 12) and white embroidery floss to stitch a pink piece to each end of the white piece.

3 Use the overcast stitch (see page 12) and pink embroidery floss to stitch the turquoise pieces next to the pink pieces.

4 Turn the bracelet over and put a strip of hot glue on the back, then attach the white backing strip so that ½ in. (1.3cm) of turquoise shows at each end.

5 Place the centers of the 10 in. (25.4cm) lengths of yarn (shown here in white) on the underside of the bracelet on the ends that hang over.

6 Glue the yarn to the ends of the bracelet and roll over the color edges to secure them. Tie the yarn ends together so that the bracelet fits your wrist.

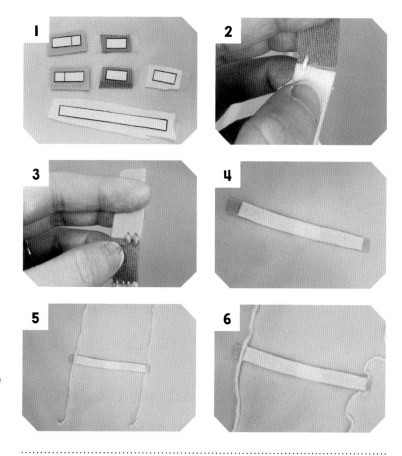

Pattern Pieces

FINISHED SIZE: 5 x ½ in. (12.7 x 1.3cm)

Pattern pieces shown at 50 percent. Photocopy at 200 percent to enlarge them to full size (see page 7).

End section Cut 2 from turquoise felt

Center section Cut 2 from pink and 1 from white felt

Base Cut 1 from white felt

Malala Yousafzai Journal Cover

Write down your thoughts, dreams, and stories in a journal covered by this Malala Yousafzai design. Let her strength remind you of the power of your own voice and keep writing—no matter what obstacles you encounter.

TOOLS & MATERIALS

- 30 x 9.5 in. (76.2 x 24cm) dark gray felt
- 13 x 6 in. (33 x 15.2cm) tan felt
- 9½ x 6½ in. (24.1 x 16.5cm) pink felt
- 3¼ x 3¼ in. (8.3 x 8.3cm) black felt
- 1 x ½ in (2.5 x 1.3cm) dark brown felt
- 16 in (40.6cm) gold rick-rack
- One no-sew magnet fastener
- Dark gray embroidery floss
- Black embroidery floss
- Pink embroidery floss
- Paper
- Paper scissors
- Tape
- Sewing scissors
- Embroidery needles
- Hot glue gun and hot glue sticks
- Tweezers (optional)

Malala Yousafzai, who was born in the Swat Valley, Pakistan, became the youngest recipient of the Nobel Peace Prize in 2014 for her campaign for girls' education. She nearly lost her life when she was shot in the head by a member of the Taliban. Malala continues her campaign for education through The Malala Fund.

1 Photocopy the pattern pieces onto paper and cut them out. Tape the pattern pieces to the felt using the colors stated.

2 Use the backstitch (see page 11) to add detail to Malala's face as follows: dark gray embroidery floss for the hair and the folds in her clothing; black for her eyes; and pink for her lips. Use the backstitch and three strands of black embroidery floss to add the nose detail to her face. Use the three strands of black embroidery floss and a French knot (see page 12) to add the mole to her chin. Cut out all the felt pieces and remove the pattern pieces except for the eyebrows and eyes.

3 Assemble the face by gluing the sections together as follows: the hair piece to the head; the eyes below the eye embroidery; and the eyebrows above the eyes. You can use tweezers to help you if you like (see page 7). Remove the remaining pattern pieces.

4 Assemble the clothing by gluing the sections together as follows: the smaller clothing piece to the larger clothing piece; the bottom only of the clothing piece to the tan body piece.

5 Assemble the face and clothing by gluing the sections together as follows: place the head on the tan body piece under the clothing piece, then glue the head to the body; the top of the clothing piece to the face and body; the rick-rack to the clothing, using the thick line on the pattern as a guide.

1

2
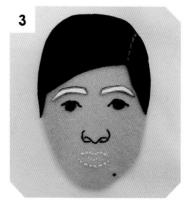

3
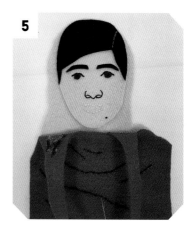

4
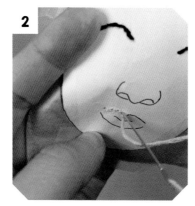

5

Journal Cover

6 Assemble the journal by placing the two cover pieces side by side and position the spine so that ½ in. (1.3cm) overlaps with the journal cover on each side. Apply a thin line of glue along the edge of the cover pieces and glue on the spine.

7 Using pink embroidery floss and the running stitch (see page 11), stitch the spine to the journal covers along the edges of the spine.

8 Position the magnet on the closure strip and attach it following the package instructions. In this example, the tabs are pushed through the felt and flattened.

9 Glue the closure strips together, ensuring the magnet is facing out. Use the running stitch and pink embroidery floss to sew the edges of the closure strip together.

10 Glue the closure strips together, ensuring the magnet is facing out. Use the running stitch and pink embroidery floss to sew the edges together and embellish them. Place the closure strip on the back of the journal cover (do not attach), fold over the journal, and use the closure strip to position the other half of the magnet on the front cover. Attach the magnet.

11 Open the journal and position the flap pockets on the inside edges. Use the running stitch and pink embroidery floss to sew around the perimeter of the journal, attaching the pockets as you do so.

12 Glue Malala to the front cover, making sure she touches but does not overlap the spine piece. Glue the closure strap to the back of the journal.

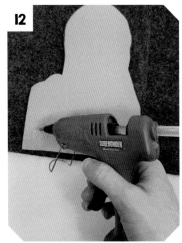

Pattern Pieces

FINISHED SIZE:

12.75 x 9 in (32.4 x 22.9cm) to fit an A5 (8 x 5½ in./20.3 x 14cm) journal

Pattern pieces shown at 20 percent. Photocopy at 500 percent to enlarge them to full size (see page 7).

Cut out the following pieces from dark gray felt for the journal cover:

2 pieces measuring 9 x 6¼ in. (22.9 x 15.9cm) for the cover

2 pieces measuring 9 x 4 in. (22.9 x 10.2cm) for the flap pockets

1 piece measuring 9 x 2¼ in. (22.9 x 5.7cm) for the spine

2 pieces measuring 4 x 1¼ in. (10.2 x 3.2cm) for the closure tab

Body
Cut 1 from tan felt

Clothing
Cut 1 of each from pink felt

Head
Cut 1 from tan felt

Hair
Cut 1 from black felt

Eyebrows
Cut 1 of each from black felt

Eyes
Cut 1 of each from dark brown felt

Maya Angelou Pencil Topper

Let one of the great feminist authors of the modern age inspire your writing as she sits atop your pencil or pen. Write along with Maya Angelou and always rise above.

TOOLS & MATERIALS

- 6½ x 1½ in. (16.5 x 3.8cm) black felt
- 5½ x 1½ in. (14 x 3.8cm) brown felt
- 1½ x 1 in. (3.8 x 2.5cm) dark gray felt
- 1 x 1 in. (2.5 x 2.5cm) light gray felt
- ½ x ½ in. (1.3 x 1.3cm) yellow felt
- 3 in. (7.6cm) yellow yarn
- Black embroidery floss
- Pink embroidery floss
- Paper
- Paper scissors
- Tape
- Sewing scissors
- Embroidery needles
- Hot glue gun and hot glue sticks
- Tweezers (optional)

American poet and civil rights activist Maya Angelou was also a singer, dancer, actress, and composer. Her best-known work is her autobiographical book *I Know Why the Caged Bird Sings*. In 2010, she received the Presidential Medal of Freedom from President Barack Obama.

1 Photocopy the pattern pieces onto paper and cut them out. Tape the pattern pieces to the felt using the colors stated. Cut out all the pieces except the head piece.

2 Use the backstitch (see page 11) to add details as follows: two strands of black embroidery floss to stitch the nose detail and two strands of pink embroidery floss to sew the lip detail. Use a French knot (see page 12) and two strands of black embroidery floss for the eyes. Remove the pattern pieces.

3 Place the brown body piece on top of the black body piece; position the shirt on top of them. Use black embroidery floss and the overcast stitch (see page 12) to stitch the layers together, leaving the bottom open.

4 Assemble the face by gluing the sections together as follows: the dark gray hair to the head; the light gray streak to the dark gray hair; the head to the main body piece; the earrings to the head; the sleeves to the shirt; and the hands to the sleeves. You can use tweezers to help you if you like (see page 7).

5 Cut a 3 in. (7.6cm) length of yarn and loop it around the neck. Glue at the back to make a necklace.

1

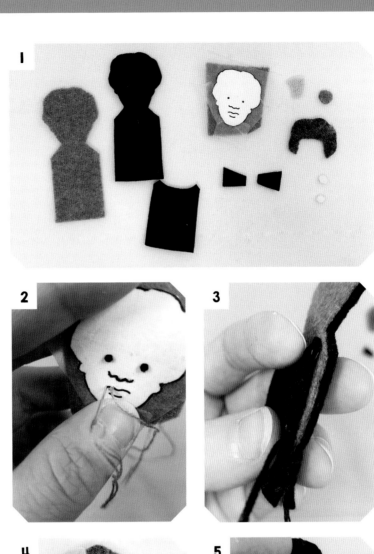

2

3

4

5

Maya Angelou Pencil Topper

Pattern Pieces

FINISHED SIZE: 2¾ x 1¼ in. (7 x 3.2cm)

Pattern pieces shown true to size.
Photocopy at 100 percent (see page 7).

Main body
Cut 1 from black
and 1 from
brown felt

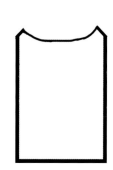

Shirt
Cut 1 from
black felt

Head
Cut 1 from
brown felt

Hair
Cut 1 from dark
gray felt

Sleeves
Cut 1 of each from
black felt

Hair streak
Cut 1 from light
gray felt

Hands
Cut 2 from
brown felt

Earrings
Cut 1 of each from
yellow felt

Goddess Crown

Celebrate your inner goddess with a circle
of regal laurel in earthy olive felt. This crown
is a symbol of victory, honor, and power.

TOOLS & MATERIALS

- 14 x 8 in. (35.6 x 20.3cm)
  olive green felt

- Plastic headband

- 12 beads

- Paper

- Paper scissors

- Sewing scissors

- Hot glue gun and hot glue sticks

In ancient
Greece, crowns of laurel
leaves were given to the
winners of athletic and poetic
competitions, while Roman
commanders wore them
as symbols of success
in battle.

Goddess Crown

1 Photocopy the pattern piece onto paper and cut it out. Tape the pattern piece to the felt and cut out a leaf. Repeat until you have 39 leaves. You may need more than one paper pattern piece.

2 Curve twelve of the leaves. To do this, place a short strip of glue on the inside tip of each leaf and pinch the sides together. The remaining twenty-seven leaves will be used flat.

3 Start to glue the flat leaves to the headband so that the leaves overlap slightly at the base.

4 Arrange the flat leaves so that they cover the headband but leave space for the curved leaves.

5 Glue the curved leaves to the headband so that they alternate with the flat leaves.

6 Glue the beads to the "stem" section of the curved leaves on alternate sides of the crown.

You can add additional adornment to your crown if you wish. For example, you can weave metallic ribbon through the leaves or add more beads.

Pattern Pieces

FINISHED SIZE: 7 x 5½ in. (17.8 x 14cm)

Pattern pieces shown true to size.
Photocopy at 100 percent (see page 7).

Leaf
Cut 39 from
olive green
felt

Backpack Badges

Adorn your backpack with a badge of pride. Whether making a statement about voting, equality, femininity, or power, these badges allow you to say a lot without speaking a word.

There are many ways to make these badges your own. Choose the colors you like and use fabric paint or stitching to embellish them.

TOOLS & MATERIALS

- 6½ x 3 in. (16.5 x 7.6cm) white felt
- 5½ x 3 in. (14 x 7.6cm) black felt
- 5½ x 3 in. (14 x 7.6cm) dark gray felt
- 4½ x 3 in. (11.4 x 7.6cm) red felt
- 4½ x 3 in. (11.4 x 7.6cm) dark pink felt
- 4½ x 3 in. (11.4 x 7.6cm) light purple felt
- 4 x 2 in. (10.2 x 5.1cm) brown felt
- 3½ x 3½ in (8.9 x 8.9cm) light pink felt
- 2½ x 2 in. (6.3 x 5cm) medium pink felt

- 2½ x 1 in. (6.3 x 2.5cm) dark purple felt
- 2 x 2 in. (5.1 x 5.1cm) dark blue felt
- 2 x 1½ in. (5.1 x 3.8cm) medium blue felt
- 2 x 1½ in. (5.1 x 3.8cm) light blue felt
- Blue embroidery floss
- Dark gray embroidery floss
- White embroidery floss
- Pink embroidery floss
- Black embroidery floss

- Pink fabric paint
- Purple fabric paint
- White fabric paint
- Paper
- Paper scissors
- Tape
- Sewing scissors
- Embroidery needles
- Hot glue gun and hot glue sticks
- Tweezers (optional)

1 Photocopy the pattern pieces onto paper and cut them out. Tape the pattern pieces to the felt using the colors stated. Cut out the felt pieces that do not have any marked stitch detail.

2 To decorate the bra badge, use the running stitch (see page 11) and blue embroidery floss to stitch the outside border on the inner circle; dark gray embroidery floss to stitch the long "ray" detail on the inner circle; and white embroidery floss to stitch the short "ray" detail on the inner circle. Remove the pattern pieces.

3 To complete the bra badge, glue the top bra piece to the bottom bra piece. Then glue the bra to the inner circle and the inner circle to the outer circle. You can use tweezers to help you if you like (see page 7).

4 To make the female symbol badge, glue the burst to the outer circle and then the symbol to the burst.

5 To decorate the fist of power badge, use the running stitch and pink embroidery floss to stitch the outside border on the inner circle. Remove the pattern pieces.

Backpack Badges

6 To assemble the fist of power badge, glue the inner circle to the outer circle. Make sure the thumb is cut on your fist piece and glue it to the inner circle (making sure not to glue the thumb piece down). Place your fingers on your fist for positioning, then glue down (do not glue fingers over thumb, put thumb over index finger). You can use tweezers to help you if you like (see page 7).

7 To complete the fist of power badge, use pink fabric paint to add the "fingernails."

8 To decorate the pad badge, use the backstitch (see page 11) and black embroidery floss to stitch detail onto the pad piece; use the running stitch and white embroidery floss to stitch the outside border on the inner circle and the outside border on the outside circle. Remove the pattern pieces.

9 To complete the pad badge, glue the inner circle to the outer circle and then the pad to the badge.

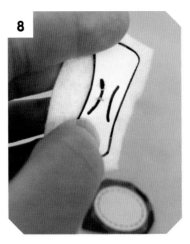

10 To assemble the underwear badge, glue the inner circle to the outer circle (you may want to save the inner circle pattern piece for design reference). Glue the top underwear to the bottom underwear and the underwear to the badge.

11 To decorate the underwear badge, use pink fabric paint to add the bow detail on the underwear and the long "ray" detail on the inner circle. Use purple fabric paint to make the short "ray" detail on the inner circle. Use white fabric paint to make the stitch detail on the outside border of the inner circle.

12 To decorate the vote badge, use white embroidery floss and the running stitch to make the stitch detail on the outer box.

13 To complete the vote badge, glue the inner box to the outer box and then the check mark to the badge.

14 Affix your badges to your backpack by using an overcast or running stitch (see pages 11 and 12) or using hot glue.

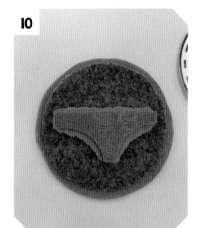

10

11

12

13

Backpack Badges

Pattern Pieces

FINISHED SIZE:

2½ in. (6.3cm) average

Pattern pieces shown at 30 percent. Photocopy at 333 percent to enlarge them to full size (see page 7).

Bra outer circle
Cut 1 from dark gray felt

Bra inner circle
Cut 1 from black felt

Under bra
Cut 1 from light blue felt

Top bra
Cut 1 from medium blue felt

Female Symbol outer circle
Cut 1 from dark pink felt

Female Symbol burst
Cut 1 from light pink felt

Female Symbol
Cut 1 from medium pink

Vote outer box
Cut 1 from dark blue felt

Fist of Power outer circle
Cut 1 from black felt

Fist of Power inner circle
Cut 1 from white felt

Fist of Power fist and fingers
Cut 1 of each from brown felt

Vote inner box
Cut 1 from white felt

Pad outer circle
Cut 1 from red felt

Pad inner circle
Cut 1 from dark pink felt

Pad
Cut 1 from white felt

Vote check mark
Cut 1 from red felt

Underwear outer circle
Cut 1 from light purple felt

Underwear inner circle
Cut 1 from dark gray felt

Underwear under piece
Cut 1 from light purple felt

Underwear top piece
Cut 1 from dark purple felt

Amelia Earhart Eyeglass Case

Strike out on an adventure—but don't forget your glasses. Stash your specs, sunglasses, or swimming goggles in a case adorned with the image of Amelia Earhart.

Pioneering aviator Amelia Earhart was the first woman to pilot a plane solo across the Atlantic Ocean. As well as many other notable successes in the air, she encouraged women to reject traditional roles and try jobs and skills usually done by men. She disappeared in 1937 during an attempt to be the first woman to fly around the world.

TOOLS & MATERIALS

- 8½ x 7½ in. (21.6 x 19cm) light blue felt
- 5½ x 3 in. (14 x 7.6cm) cream felt
- 5½ x 3 in. (14 x 7.6cm) brown felt
- 2½ x 1½ in. (6.3 x 3.8cm) dark gray felt
- 2½ x 1½ in. (6.3 x 3.8cm) light gray felt
- Black embroidery floss
- Pink embroidery floss
- Blue embroidery floss
- Paper
- Paper scissors
- Tape
- Sewing scissors
- Embroidery needles
- Hot glue gun and hot glue sticks
- Tweezers (optional)
- Pins

Amelia Earhart Eyeglass Case

1 Photocopy the pattern pieces onto paper and cut them out. Tape the pattern pieces to the felt using the colors stated.

2 Use the backstitch (see page 11) to add details as follows: black embroidery floss to make eyelid and nose detail; and pink embroidery floss to make the lip detail. Use black embroidery floss and a French knot (see page 12) to make the eyes. Cut out all the felt pieces. Remove the pattern pieces.

3 To assemble the Amelia Earhart motif, glue the cap to her head; then the lenses to the aviator glasses; and finally the glasses to the cap. You can use tweezers to help you if you like (see page 7).

4 Fold the eyeglass case piece in half and pin the edges together to hold them. Use blue embroidery floss and the blanket stitch (see page 13) to sew the edges of the case together (leaving the top straight edge open).

5 Glue the Amelia Earhart motif to the front of the eyeglass case.

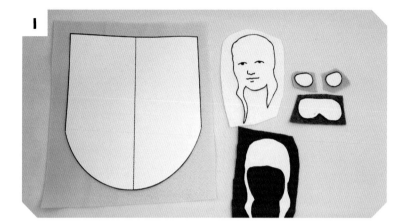

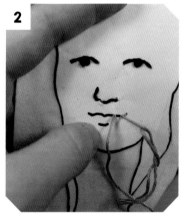

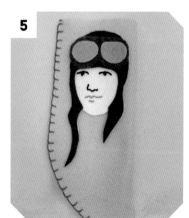

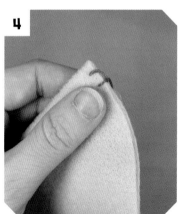

Pattern Pieces

FINISHED SIZE: 8⅜ x 3⅝ in. (21.3 x 9.2cm)

Pattern pieces shown at 50 percent.
Photocopy at 200 percent to enlarge
them to full size (see page 7).

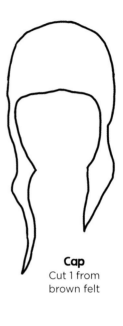

Cap
Cut 1 from
brown felt

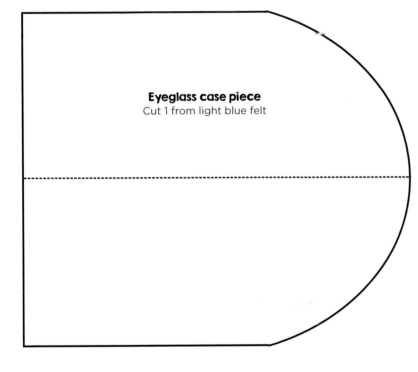

Eyeglass case piece
Cut 1 from light blue felt

Lenses
Cut 1 of each from
light gray felt

**Aviator
glasses**
Cut 1 from dark
gray felt

Face
Cut 1 from
cream felt

Letter to Myself

Write a letter to yourself and keep it in this envelope—open it in a year to see what you've accomplished, or whenever you need a reminder of how awesome you are.

TOOLS & MATERIALS

- 9 x 8 in. (22.9 x 20.3cm) pink felt
- 9 x 8 in. (22.9 x 20.3cm) blue felt
- 2 x 1 in. (5.1 x 2.5cm) purple felt
- 2 buttons
- Hook-and-loop fastening tape
- Pink embroidery floss
- Purple embroidery floss
- Paper
- Paper scissors
- Tape
- Sewing scissors
- Embroidery needles
- Hot glue gun and hot glue sticks
- Tweezers (optional)

There are two versions of the envelope; one features embroidery and a button closure, and the other uses glue to attach the decorations and has a hook-and-loop tape closure. Use the letter inside to describe who you are right now and to answer these questions: Who do you think you'll be in the future? What do you like? What are your goals? What do you love about yourself?

To Make the Embroidered Envelope

1 Photocopy the pattern pieces onto paper and cut them out. Tape the pattern pieces to the felt using the colors stated.

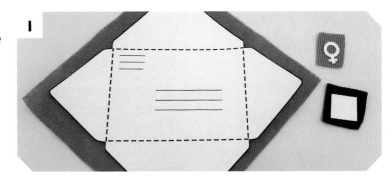

2 Use the backstitch (see page 11) and pink embroidery floss to stitch the detailing on the front of the envelope. Cut out the envelope. Remove the pattern pieces.

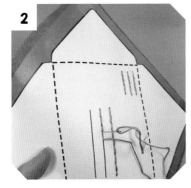
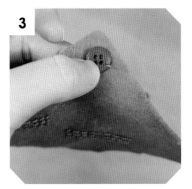

3 Stitch a button to the top flap of the envelope (it will be facing up and out when the felt is held flat).

4 Fold the lower flap back and up. Put a thin line of glue on the edges of either side to glue the inner flaps in.

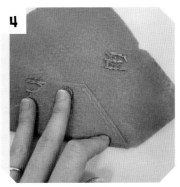

5 Fold the top flap down to help you decide where you should stitch your second button. Sew the second button onto the back lower half of the envelope.

6 Tie a 12-in. (30.5cm) length of embroidery floss around the lower button and loop it around the upper button to seal the envelope.

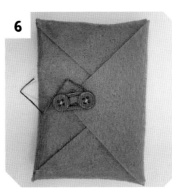
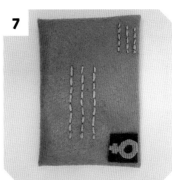

7 Glue the female symbol to the stamp and then glue the stamp to the envelope. You can use tweezers to help you if you like (see page 7).

Letter to Myself

To Make the Glued Envelope

8 Photocopy the pattern pieces onto paper and cut them out. Tape the pattern pieces to the felt using the colors stated. Cut out the felt. Remove the pattern pieces.

9 Fold the lower flap back and up. Put a thin line of glue on the edges of either side to glue the inner flaps in.

10 Glue the loop side of a tab of hook-and-loop fastener to the underside of the upper flap.

11 Fold the upper flap over to determine the position of the hook-and-loop fastener on the lower half of the envelope. Glue the hook side of a tab of hook-and-loop fastener to the lower half of the envelope.

12 Glue the symbol to the stamp and then glue the stamp to the envelope. You can use tweezers to help you if you like (see page 7).

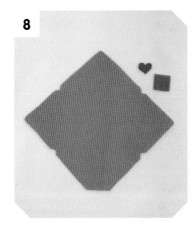

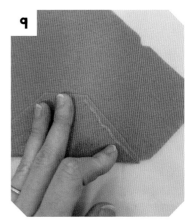

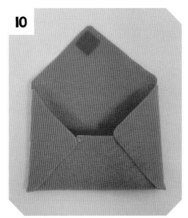

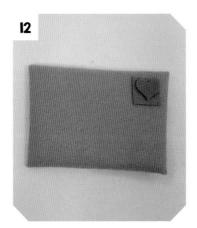

Pattern Pieces

FINISHED SIZE: 4½ x 3½ in. (11.4 x 8.9cm)

Pattern pieces shown at 60 percent. Photocopy at 167 percent to enlarge them to full size (see page 7).

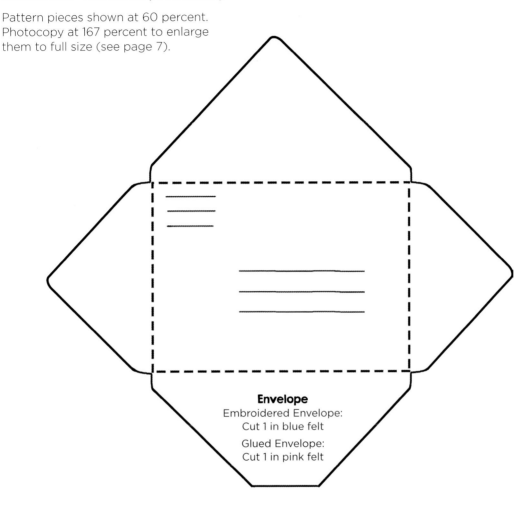

Envelope
Embroidered Envelope:
Cut 1 in blue felt

Glued Envelope:
Cut 1 in pink felt

Stamp
Embroidered Envelope:
Cut 1 in purple felt

Glued Envelope:
Cut 1 in blue felt

Female Symbol
Embroidered
Envelope:
Cut 1 in pink felt

Heart
Glued Envelope:
Cut 1 in
purple felt

Fortuna Coin Keeper Key Chain

What better place to stash your cash than under the watch of Fortuna—Roman goddess of fortune and luck.

Keep this snappy little coin pocket on your key chain or on a zipper pull so you will always have a few coins of fortune with you when you need them. The motif combines Fortuna's face with a cornucopia—a traditional symbol of plenty.

TOOLS & MATERIALS

- 10 x 4½ in. (25.4 x 11.4cm) black felt
- 3 x 3 in. (7.6 x 7.6cm) light gray felt
- 2½ x 2 in. (6.3 x 5cm) dark gray felt
- Black embroidery floss
- One size 2 snap fastener
- One ¼ in. (0.6cm) eyelet
- Jump ring
- Sequins
- Paper
- Paper scissors
- Tape
- Sewing scissors
- Chalk
- Embroidery needle
- Hot glue gun and hot glue sticks
- Tweezers (optional)
- Eyelet kit

1 Photocopy the pattern pieces onto paper and cut them out. Tape the pattern pieces to the felt using the colors stated. Cut out the felt and save a 1 in. (2.5cm) square of black felt for the snap fastener. Remove the pattern pieces.

2 Place the case pieces together with the wrong sides of the felt facing outward. Use chalk to mark the lines where you'll be stitching.

3 Use the backstitch (see page 11) and black embroidery floss to stitch around the perimeter of the case.

4 Turn the case right-side-out. Place the stud side of the snap on the top of the back piece of the case (the piece without a flap). Use the flap as a guide to position the snap. Stitch the snap onto the case.

5 Stitch the socket side of the snap onto the saved square of black felt.

6 Snap the socket side of the snap to the stud side sewn to the case. Apply glue to the back of the felt and fold the flap over to position the snap.

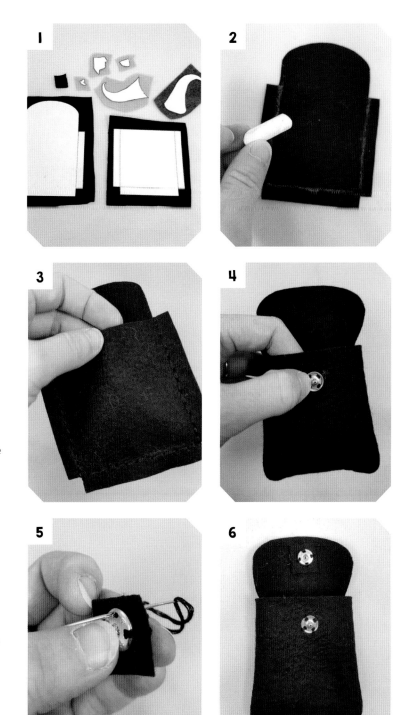

Fortuna Coin Keeper Key Chain

7 Glue the light gray cornucopia piece onto the dark gray piece. Position the Fortuna and cornucopia pieces on the front of the coin pocket and glue in place. You can use tweezers to help you if you like (see page 7).

8 Decide where you want the eyelet for the jump ring to go. Mark the position with chalk.

9 Make a small cut in the front and back layers of the coin pocket, taking care not to cut into the flap.

10 Attach the eyelet following the package instructions.

11 Glue on the sequins and attach the jump ring through the eyelet.

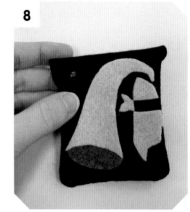

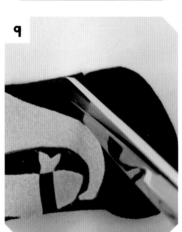

Pattern Pieces

FINISHED SIZE: 4 x 3 in. (10.2 x 7.6cm)

Pattern pieces shown at 60 percent.
Photocopy at 167 percent to enlarge
them to full size (see page 7).

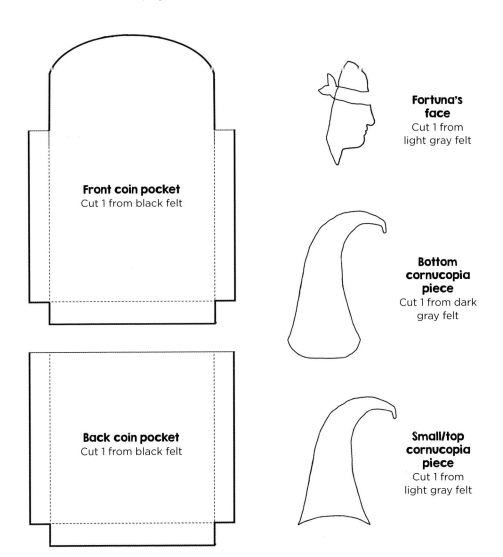

Front coin pocket
Cut 1 from black felt

Back coin pocket
Cut 1 from black felt

Fortuna's face
Cut 1 from
light gray felt

Bottom cornucopia piece
Cut 1 from dark
gray felt

Small/top cornucopia piece
Cut 1 from
light gray felt

Index

Acknowledgments

I'd like to thank Derrick for his support, Nadia for her assistance and project testing, and Simone for her patience and naps. My family for their help and my parents for their grandparenting. Also, the MTJMs for their advice and encouragement. Special thanks to the great team at Toucan: Sarah Bloxham, Julie Brooke, Ellen Dupont, and Leah Germann.

Toucan Books Ltd. would like to thank Autumn and Florence Green for their help.